MATCH!
THE BEST FOOTBALL MAGAZINE!

REAL MADRID ANNUAL 2018

Written by
Stephen Fishlock, Jamie Evans & Ben Wier

Designed by
Darryl Tooth & Calum Booth

CONTENTS

A Pillar Box Red Publication

in association with

THE BEST FOOTBALL MAGAZINE!

ISBN: 978-1-907823-87-9

RONALDO '100 GOALS'

Last season, *CRISTIANO RONALDO* became the first player to score 100 goals in the Champions League. Check out how he got there...

GOAL '16 **GOAL '17**

Zurich	2	5	Real Madrid

September, 2009 Ronaldo's first CL goals in a Real shirt came in his first game in the competition for his new club. The FW's ability to make the ball dip through the air from free-kicks was already legendary, and he proved it in Switzerland with two excellent strikes.

GOAL 28

Tottenham 0 | 1 **Real Madrid**

April, 2011 Ronaldo's first goal on English soil since leaving the Prem was helped in by a Heurelho Gomes error, but it did set up a Clasico semi-final. It was to be his final goal of the tournament, as Barcelona went through to beat his old club Man. United in the final.

GOAL 29

Real Madrid 3 | 0 **Ajax**

September, 2011 A flowing team move involving Karim Benzema, Mesut Ozil and Kaka brought Ron his first goal of the 2011-12 campaign. After an Ajax attack broke down, the four players flew forward with pace, with CR7 eventually tapping in a cross from the right.

GOAL 37
GOAL 38

Real Madrid 2 | 1 **Bayern**

April, 2012 Another CL semi-final brought more heartbreak for Cristiano, despite scoring two goals in the second leg against Bayern. Having lost the first match 2-1, the No.7's goals took the match to penalties, but his spot-kick was saved by keeper Manuel Neuer.

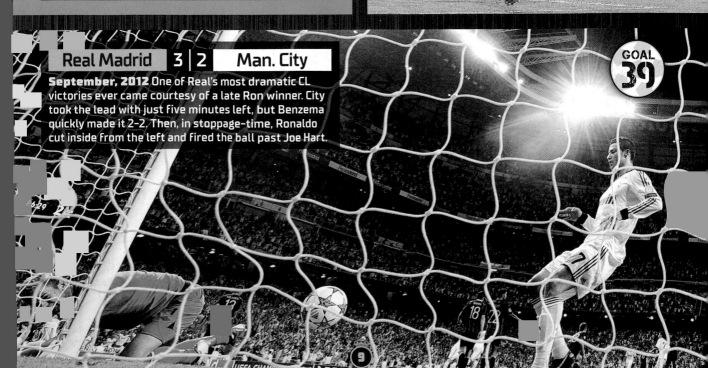

Real Madrid 3 | 2 **Man. City**

September, 2012 One of Real's most dramatic CL victories ever came courtesy of a late Ron winner. City took the lead with just five minutes left, but Benzema quickly made it 2-2. Then, in stoppage-time, Ronaldo cut inside from the left and fired the ball past Joe Hart.

GOAL 39

GOAL 40

GOAL 41

GOAL 42

Ajax	1	4	Real Madrid

October, 2012 The first of seven CL hat-tricks for Ron came in Amsterdam with three classy finishes, but the third was the pick of the bunch. After being played through by Sami Khedira, he coolly lifted the ball over the onrushing keeper with a perfect left-foot lob.

GOAL 46

Man. United	1	2	Real Madrid

March, 2013 This 2013 round of 16 clash was emotional for CR7, as he returned to the club where he made his name. After scoring in the 1-1 draw in the first leg, he was given a hero's welcome at Old Trafford, even after scoring the goal that knocked out ten-man United!

GOAL 50

Dortmund	4	1	Real Madrid

April, 2013 Reaching 50 CL goals would normally be a special night, but this quickly turned into a nightmare for Ronaldo! His first-half goal had brought Los Blancos level, but a four-goal haul for Robert Lewandowski all but dumped the La Liga giants out of Europe!

GOAL 59

Copenhagen	0	2	Real Madrid

December, 2013 Cristiano was determined to win the CL in a white shirt, and began 2013-14 in top form. A tidy finish in Denmark not only took Real through their group in top spot, it also took CR7 forward to nine group stage net-busters – a record at the time!

UNITED GOALS

CR7 already had 15 Champions League goals on the board when he joined Real...

Man. United	7
Roma	1

GOAL 1
GOAL 2
April, 2007 His first CL goals came in this demolition of Roma in the 2007 quarters! He drilled in the first with his right foot, then tapped in a second.

Sporting	0
Man. United	1

GOAL 4
September, 2007 His first game back at Sporting since leaving the club was a touching night for Ronaldo, and he chose not to celebrate after his header won the game for United.

Roma	0
Man. United	2

GOAL 10
April, 2008 The Italians put up more of a fight in 2008, but still couldn't contain Cristiano, as the No.7's towering header helped United on their way to a second semi-final in a row.

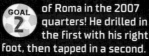

Bayern 0 | 4 Real Madrid

April, 2014 Real were at their counter-attacking best to defeat Pep Guardiola's Bayern in the semis, and Ron was key to the win. His first goal finished off a move that went from one penalty area to the other in the blink of an eye, while his second was a clever free-kick!

GOAL 65

GOAL 66

GOAL 67

Real Madrid 4 | 1 Atletico Madrid

May, 2014 The first all-Madrid final saw Cristiano finally get his hands on the famous trophy for Real, and naturally he got himself on the score sheet. His penalty in the final minute of extra-time was his 17th of the campaign – a record for both himself and the comp!

GOAL 70

Liverpool 0 | 3 Real Madrid

October, 2014 A frosty reception awaited Ronaldo at Anfield in the 2014-15 group stage, but it didn't stop him scoring one of his finest CL goals! After some quick passing, a chipped ball from James Rodriguez picked him out in the box to put it in on the half-volley.

Chelsea	1		Porto	0		Arsenal	1
Man. United	1		Man. United	1		Man. United	3

GOAL 11 **May, 2008** The first all-English final was decided on penalties, but not before Ron had opened the scoring with another perfectly-timed header – his 42nd goal that season!

GOAL 13 **April, 2009** This epic thunderbolt was possibly his best goal in a red shirt. 35 yards out, the forward turned and smashed the ball into the top corner to send United into the semis.

GOAL 14 **May, 2009** In his final season at United, Ronaldo fired them into another CL Final with two goals at The Emirates – the second,

GOAL 15 a classic counter-attack strike!

GOAL 72

Real Madrid	4	0	Ludogorets

December, 2014 Plenty of Ron's goals have been more important than this penalty, but few have been as historic. His 72nd CL goal took him past Real legend Raul in the competition's list of all-time top scorers, and closer to the all-time leader at the time, Lionel Messi!

GOAL 73

Schalke	0	2	Real Madrid

February, 2015 The Madrid legend set another remarkable record in the first leg of the last 16 clash with Schalke. His towering header in the first half meant that he'd scored in 12 consecutive Champions League away games, a record which still stands!

GOAL 78
GOAL 79
GOAL 80

Real Madrid	4	0	Shakhtar

September, 2015 After losing another semi-final, the Portugal goal king bounced back for the 2015-16 campaign with a devastating performance. His third Champions League hat-trick took him three goals clear of Messi as the competition's all-time highest scorer!

GOAL 85
GOAL 86
GOAL 87
GOAL 88

Real Madrid	8	0	Malmo

December, 2015 His first ever four-goal haul in the Champo League brought even more records. As well as matching the biggest ever group stage win, the No.7 also became the first player to reach double figures before the knockout stages, finishing with 11 goals!

GOAL STATS!

Check out the stats behind Ronaldo's epic 100 Champions League goals...

HOW?
17 Header
15 Left Foot
68 Right Foot

WHEN?
3 Extra Time
45 First Half
52 Second Half

TYPE?
11 Penalties
12 Free-Kicks
77 Open Play

WHERE?
16 Outside Penalty Area
25 Six-Yard box
59 Inside Penalty Area

GOAL 91

GOAL 92

GOAL 93

| Real Madrid | 3 | 0 | Wolfsburg |

April, 2016 Wolfsburg shocked Real with a 2-0 win in the first leg of this quarter-final, and the Spanish giants needed their star man at his best in the second leg. His superb hat-trick helped fire them through to the semis on their way to lifting the trophy once more!

GOAL 94

| Real Madrid | 2 | 1 | Sporting |

September, 2016 This inch-perfect FK was marked with an apologetic wave to his former fans, as Ronaldo chose not to celebrate against his old club once again. The goal, an 89th-minute equaliser, proved to be the catalyst for a key comeback as Real went on to win 2-1.

GOAL 98

GOAL 99

GOAL 100

| Real Madrid | 4 | 2 | Bayern |

April, 2017 What better way to reach goal 100 than with a hat-trick in front of your home fans? Having taken the game to extra-time, Bayern believed they could progress. But once again Ron made the difference with a world-class performance, and a world-class treble!

HOME OR AWAY?

2 Neutral Venue

47 Away

51 Home

WHICH TEAMS?

6 Galatasaray, Malmo

9 Bayern

7 Ajax, Schalke

WHICH GOALIES?

5 Buffon, Pyatov, Vermeer

9 Neuer, Wiland

6 Muslera

ASSISTED BY?

6 Marcelo

11 Benzema

7 Bale

WORDSEARCH

Can you find the names of all these expensive Real signings?

```
W C W T C G H X O S P G B E R N X D U M X C C M H K W Q F P
E F A D A N I L O P M I E X H P M A J F J F L A U W F Y I L
S T M A B U P J M D E H W I V A L I H V O C L S U J R I Y A
S I K A S S Q D V Z F A O P H T F U N Y O L O E M O Q U D M
P J H O S Q N D R T N Q K K U V E K R U P O V L I H S N Q L
K E C W V T M P N O O T C M O A J H O V R J N N G D U N E P
C P N U P A U M L B B E X F Y C I H L K F A U R H F N N I R
B D E U V D C G T G B B J T X C P U N C Y J K O Z Z Y K J S
U M X P L K N I Q P O N E L Z G J V V Y B O D N K O G D W K
N O R Q L K Q M C S L L Z N L F D P I B I U B A H R A P R E
N D G L C O E N T R A O G K X U C J S M M X Y L O O M Z A O
C R Y T X N E S P R X M P A M M D K C I U D W D R B W U F I
B I Q R K M D Z Q D R C U N Z Q G A O S R F N O B I Q V Z J
K C M R Q B B J H N V L E E D R M K D W N O I M L N N E X D
E T R C I K U K T H U J Q K L C Z A M X O F B E U H O D T S
A J M L J F A B U M I O B B H J X I S R A M O S B O U W P B
W L Y E A N E L K A W M B U V K G X H X U V S D I M A R I A
U P J Z N C S Z I R L P H X F C P W I B S W U D A U M R L O
I D N Z J X X L V B H X A Z C I T T R D I S K A G Z C Y O L
W P Q S I L L A R R A M E N D I Y L A M O R A T A S C S D S
C F D I Y W B H C F I G O W G W Z G B A D M D T G P N O V Q
V K M A X B K M B H I V G Q L R E F T C T P I P S O S O B Y
M V R F Q C O N C E I C A O A L K S B I T Z A D L T N I Y B
B G V Z Z Z H H G P E P E A D U I C T I O B R A S I E X O T
F I W L Z E E B A L E M L D P T D O X Y J Q R T D J I H E D
I L P D I R P A Z L Q E J T P F W J F C G H A V I F J O L R
B E N Z E M A X B A T E O A U G M U C X Q S A I Z I D A N E
L S A H M R D Q J N U V B V M S H W S G O C Q Z Y B E Y O C
T S Y M A X R L U C W A L U N E H E A D Y V E E D O R H F B
K I B G Z L S H V A K K Q G R E S Y G X V S F I T I L O M W
```

Alonso	Coentrao	Huntelaar	Kovacic	Robben
Anelka	Conceicao	Illarramendi	Kroos	Robinho
Bale	Danilo	Isco	Modric	Ronaldo
Baptista	Di Maria	James	Morata	Samuel
Beckham	Diarra	Junior	Pepe	Sneijder
Benzema	Figo	Kaka	Ramos	Zidane

SPOT THE DIFFERENCE

Study these Real Madrid v Barcelona pictures really carefully, then see if you can find the ten differences between them!

ANSWERS ON PAGE 60

BALE
BEST OF BRITAIN

The Wales wizard is the UK's most successful football export.

When Real Madrid broke the world transfer record for the fifth time in their history to sign Gareth Bale, it completed a remarkable journey for the Cardiff lad. Just four years previously, he had been struggling to get a game as a left-back for Tottenham, while carrying the unwanted record of playing 24 games in a row without winning a Premier League game. His transformation from a young LB with potential to one of the most devastating attackers in the world has been incredible, and there's no denying that he could get even better. Alongside goal machines Cristiano Ronaldo and Karim Benzema, his role in 'BBC' has been crucial to the La Liga giants' recent success. His trophy cabinet at Real is bulging, and is only going to get bigger and bigger over the next few seasons...

THE NEW RONALDO

The negotiations for the Wales megastar's transfer went on throughout the summer of 2013, but the deal was finally confirmed at the end of the window. In moving from the Premier League for a record-breaking amount, the comparisons with Ronaldo were obvious. But the pair of powerful forwards have learned to link up well and form a devastating partnership together.

SPEED DEMON

A series of injuries limited Bale in his first season, but he announced himself as a star in the 2014 Copa del Rey Final. With the game locked at 1-1 and heading for extra-time, the ace forward unleashed his pace down the left wing. Bale practically had to run into the crowd pitchside to avoid Barça defenders, but had the speed to reach the ball and poke home a ridiculous winner.

CHAMPO LEAGUE LEGEND

If the goal against Barcelona had made him popular amongst Real's fans, he became a true hero a few weeks later. It was his class extra-time header against Atletico Madrid in the 2014 Champions League Final that really took the game away from Real's city rivals, and sent Los Blancos on their way to 'La Decima' and their first European trophy in 12 years. The scenes!

BRITISH HISTORY MAKER

Bale's performances and status at the world's biggest club have elevated him to the very top of the game, and he is now considered British football's greatest export. In March 2016, he scored his 43rd La Liga goal on the way to a 4-0 win over Sevilla, to go past Gary Lineker as the league's all-time top scoring British player. Winning everything going has helped his cause, too!

REAL TROPHY CABINET

3x Champions Leagues

1x La Liga

1x Club World Cup

1x Copa del Rey

1x Spanish Super Cup

3x European Super Cups

BERNABEU

Get the lowdown on the mind-blowing home of the La Liga giants!

THE NAME

Los Blancos' awesome stadium was named after club legend Santiago Bernabeu, who spent 56 years at Real as a player, manager and president. Under his leadership, the ground was built and developed into one of the biggest arenas in the world. Hero!

Official Name: *Estadio Santiago Bernabeu*

Capacity: *81,044*

Year Built: *1947*

First Match: *Real Madrid 3-1 Belenenses December 14, 1947*

Record Crowd: *124,000 Real Madrid 2-0 Fiorentina May 30, 1957*

FACTPACK

THE CAPACITY

A mind-blowing 124,000 people watched Real win the 1957 European Cup at the ground. While the capacity has decreased since then, it still remains one of the greatest stadiums in world football.

SEASON REVIEW

The 2016–17 season was one of the most successful campaigns in REAL MADRID's already stellar history…

AUGUST

The players celebrate the club's third European Super Cup

Real's competitive season began in Norway against Sevilla for the European Super Cup. With Cristiano Ronaldo still recovering from his injury at Euro 2016, young gun Marco Asensio started for the first time, and made an impact within 21 minutes. Collecting the ball from 25 yards out, the attacking midfielder curled a delightful shot into the top corner to put his team in front.

The Europa League champs were far from beaten however and, after equalising just before half time, took the lead from the spot in the second half. With the clock ticking down, Sergio Ramos was on hand to rescue his team with a stoppage-time equaliser. With Sevilla reduced to ten men in extra-time, Real began to dominate, and the winner finally came from an epic solo goal from Dani Carvajal to seal the club's first trophy of the season. Los Blancos started the La Liga campaign with two wins, too.

REAL'S RESULTS

09/08	USC	Real Madrid	3-2	Sevilla
21/08	PRD	Real Sociedad	0-3	Real Madrid
27/08	PRD	Real Madrid	2-1	Celta Vigo

SEPTEMBER

Ron crashes the ball home against his old club

Back to full fitness, Ronaldo needed just six minutes to open his account for the season against Osasuna, as Real continued their 100% start in La Liga. Four days later he was on target again. With 89 minutes on the clock, Real were trailing by a goal against Sporting in the CL, when CR7 stepped up to fire home a free-kick against his former club. A few minutes later, the comeback was complete with an ace James Rodriguez header. A 2-0 victory at Espanyol the following weekend was to be Real's final win of the month.

In two games in a row, they threw away 2-1 leads in the closing minutes of the game to settle for draws against Las Palmas and Dortmund. Pressure on!

REAL'S RESULTS

Date	Comp	Home	Score	Away
10/09	PRD	Real Madrid	5-2	Osasuna
14/09	UCL	Real Madrid	2-1	Sporting
18/09	PRD	Espanyol	0-2	Real Madrid
21/09	PRD	Real Madrid	1-1	Villarreal
24/09	PRD	Las Palmas	2-2	Real Madrid
27/09	UCL	Dortmund	2-2	Real Madrid

OCTOBER

Real's winless run continued into October, as the month began with a shock draw at home to Eibar. Gareth Bale's 50th La Liga goal proved to be the only positive on a bad day, as a team missing Ramos and Luka Modric came in for heavy criticism.

However, another international break proved to be the perfect cure for Real's struggles. They were back to their best in Betis, taking a 4-0 lead inside the first half and moving to second in the table. The Whites took their impressive goalscoring form into the Champions League three days later, before stretching their unbeaten run to 24 games at home to Athletic Bilbao and returning to the top of the La Liga table.

The good times continued against third-tier Cultural Leonesa, before another Ronaldo hat-trick at Alaves rounded off a perfect month.

50 up for the Wales dragon

REAL'S RESULTS

Date	Comp	Home	Score	Away
02/10	PRD	Real Madrid	1-1	Eibar
15/10	PRD	Real Betis	1-6	Real Madrid
18/10	UCL	Real Madrid	5-1	Legia Warsaw
23/10	PRD	Real Madrid	2-1	Athletic Bilbao
26/10	CDR	Cultural Leonesa	1-7	Real Madrid
29/10	PRD	Alaves	1-4	Real Madrid

NOVEMBER

Real play in front of fan-less stadium at Legia

Real's trip to Warsaw started brilliantly when Bale scored one of the goals of the tournament inside the first minute. His 25-yard volley almost tore the net off, and when the Wales hero assisted Benzema 30 minutes later, the three points seemed wrapped up. But Legia had other plans, and produced a stunning comeback to take the lead in the 83rd minute. The Polish champs were in serious danger of ruining boss Zinedine Zidane's 100th game in charge of Los Blancos, until Mateo Kovacic's late equaliser spared his coach's blushes.

Bale made it three goals in two matches at home to Leganes the following weekend, before another international break and the first Madrid derby of the season. Following their Champions League final defeat just months before, arch rivals Atletico were determined to win in their final La Liga derby at the Vicente Calderon. The hosts were blown away, though – another Ron treble took the forward clear of Alfredo Di Stefano as the derby's all-time top scorer, and Real nine points clear of their city rivals. With the Clasico approaching, the battle for the La Liga title was fast becoming a two-horse race.

REAL'S RESULTS

02/11	UCL	Legia Warsaw	3-3	Real Madrid
06/11	PRD	Real Madrid	3-0	Leganes
19/11	PRD	Atletico Madrid	0-3	Real Madrid
22/11	UCL	Sporting	1-2	Real Madrid
26/11	PRD	Real Madrid	2-1	Sporting Gijon
30/11	CDR	Real Madrid	6-1	Cultural Leonesa

DECEMBER

Mariano celebrates his first Real goal

Trailing by six points, the pressure was all on Barça going into the first Clasico of the season, and the hosts took the lead through Luis Suarez in the second half. A key victory in the title race looked on the cards, until Ramos produced another crucial goal in stoppage-time. Four days later they faced Dortmund, needing a win to guarantee top spot in their Champions League group. However, this time it was their turn to suffer a late equaliser. After goals from Benzema and Pierre-Emerick Aubameyang, Marco Reus struck in the 88th minute to bring Real's bid to retain the trophy into serious doubt.

The following weekend, the late goals and drama continued. Closing in on a club record run of 35 matches unbeaten, Real found themselves trailing 2-1 at home to Deportivo with 84 minutes on the

clock. It was an unlikely hero that came to the rescue, as substitute Mariano bagged his first ever La Liga goal. Moments later the winner arrived in familiar fashion, as Real captain Ramos headed in a stoppage-time corner to ensure Real would finish 2016 top of La Liga.

Los Blancos' year ended in Japan in the best way possible. Goals from net-busters Benzema and Ronaldo took them past Mexican club America in the Club World Cup semi-final, and although they needed extra-time to defeat Kashima Antlers of Japan, the forward pair were on fire again in the final. Another hat-trick from Ronaldo gave him his third trophy of 2016, and the club's third too.

REAL'S RESULTS

03/12	PRD	Barcelona	1-1	Real Madrid
07/12	UCL	Real Madrid	2-2	Dortmund
10/12	PRD	Real Madrid	3-2	Deportivo
15/12	FCW	Club America	0-2	Real Madrid
18/12	FCW	Real Madrid	4-2	Kashima Antlers

JANUARY

Skipper Sergio Ramos finds his own net

2017 got off to the perfect start with eight goals in two games, but trouble was just around the corner. The warning signs came in the second leg of the Copa del Rey clash with Sevilla. Real showed their resilience once again with a dramatic comeback, scoring twice in the last ten minutes to maintain their unbeaten run, but their luck ran out in the same stadium three days later. After another late goal from Ramos – this time into his own net – had levelled the scores, a stoppage-time winner from Stevan Jovetic stunned the club from the capital. Not only did the defeat end their record-breaking 40-match unbeaten run, it brought Sevilla within a point of the league leaders, and right into the title race.

After such a long run without defeat, two came along in the same week with Celta Vigo silencing The Bernabeu in the Copa del Rey. Luck was on their side on the final weekend of the month, though – the rest of the top four all dropped points as Los Blancos swept to a comfortable victory over Real Sociedad, and moved four points ahead with a game in hand on their rivals.

REAL'S RESULTS

Date	Comp	Home	Score	Away
04/01	CDR	Real Madrid	3-0	Sevilla
07/01	PRD	Real Madrid	5-0	Granada
12/01	CDR	Sevilla	3-3	Real Madrid
15/01	PRD	Sevilla	2-1	Real Madrid
18/01	CDR	Real Madrid	1-2	Celta Vigo
21/01	PRD	Real Madrid	2-1	Malaga
25/01	CDR	Celta Vigo	2-2	Real Madrid
29/01	PRD	Real Madrid	3-0	Real Sociedad

FEBRUARY

Nothing could stop Casemiro's epic volley

REAL'S RESULTS

Date	Comp	Home	Score	Away
11/02	PRD	Osasuna	1-3	Real Madrid
15/02	UCL	Real Madrid	3-1	Napoli
18/02	PRD	Real Madrid	2-0	Espanyol
22/02	PRD	Valencia	2-1	Real Madrid
26/02	PRD	Villarreal	2-3	Real Madrid

Despite finishing second in the group, the CL draw was kind to Real as they faced Italian side Napoli. Lorenzo Insigne gave them an early scare after a mistake by Keylor Navas, but Benzema's powerful header equalised ten minutes later. Toni Kroos put them in front in the second half, before a moment of magic from Casemiro. His thumping volley from 25 yards out was one of the goals of the tournament, and gave his team a foot in the quarter-finals.

After missing three months through injury, Bale returned to the line-up and the score sheet as Real kept up the pace at the top of La Liga with a 2-0 win over Espanyol. However, the winger could do nothing to prevent their second defeat of the season at Valencia. The league leaders bossed possession, but a Ronaldo header on his 700th game for the club was not enough, and offered a glimmer of hope to the chasing pack. Disaster almost struck again at Villarreal the following weekend, but this team just doesn't know when it's beaten. Trailing 2-0 after an hour, goals from Bale, Ronaldo and Morata were enough to seal the three points and keep them top.

Ron bags a trademark header against Valencia

MARCH

Bale is given his marching orders

March began with one of the most surprising results of the season. Their ability to rescue points from another losing position couldn't overcome the disappointment of trailing 3-1 to Las Palmas, who had lost five games in a row, nor the frustration of losing Bale to suspension, after the speed demon was sent off for a rash challenge. Most disappointingly of all, the result allowed Barcelona to go top of the league. After wrapping up their place in the Champions League quarter-finals with another comfortable win in Napoli, Real were drawn against ex-manager Carlo Ancelotti and Bayern Munich. With a clash against his old mentor still a few weeks away, Zidane turned his attention to regaining top spot. More dropped points by Barça meant that wins over Real Betis and Athletic Bilbao gave Real a two-point lead and a game in hand over their fierce La Liga rivals going into the international break.

REAL'S RESULTS

01/03	PRD	Real Madrid	3-3	Las Palmas
04/03	PRD	Eibar	1-4	Real Madrid
07/03	UCL	Napoli	1-3	Real Madrid
12/03	PRD	Real Madrid	2-1	Real Betis
18/03	PRD	Athletic Bilbao	1-2	Real Madrid

Ramos is on the score sheet again

APRIL

Who else but Ronaldo?

Two more wins at the start of April set the team up for their most important run of fixtures of the season. With Atletico, Bayern and Barça all to play in the space a few weeks, it was crunch time. Trailing the leaders by ten points, Atleti were out of the La Liga race ahead of the second derby of the season, but had every intention of ruining their rivals' title challenge. And they almost did so, too. Antoine Griezmann's 85th-minute equaliser denied the hosts a deserved victory, but defeat for Barcelona elsewhere meant that the advantage stayed with Real.

After securing a crucial win in Munich, Zidane chose to rest several stars for the trip to Gijon, and was almost punished. Yet they were rescued again, this time by Isco, whose two goals bagged the points and showed just how important a player he was. The Spain star kept his place for the second leg against Bayern Munich, where Ronaldo proved to be the hero. After Bayern had forced extra-time, C-Ron rose to the occasion. His hat-trick took him to 100 CL goals, and Real to their seventh consecutive CL semi-final.

More drama was to follow, as Barça visited needing a win to stay in the title race. In one of the most incredible Clasicos of recent years, Lionel Messi scored his 500th goal for his team in injury-time to seal a dramatic win, and take them back to the top of La Liga. The momentum had shifted to the Nou Camp, but the title was still in Real's hands – win every game, and it would be theirs.

REAL'S RESULTS

02/04	PRD	Real Madrid	3-0	Alaves
05/04	PRD	Leganes	2-4	Real Madrid
08/04	PRD	Real Madrid	1-1	Atletico Madrid
12/04	UCL	Bayern Munich	1-2	Real Madrid
15/04	PRD	Sporting Gijon	2-3	Real Madrid
18/04	UCL	Real Madrid	4-2	Bayern Munich
23/04	PRD	Real Madrid	2-3	Barcelona
26/04	PRD	Deportivo	2-6	Real Madrid
29/04	PRD	Real Madrid	2-1	Valencia

A third CL trophy in four years for Los Blancos

For the fourth season in a row, the two Madrid clubs faced each other in the Champions League. With the title out of sight, Atleti were fully focused on getting revenge for the previous season's final defeat. Yet they were totally helpless against an unstoppable performance from Ronaldo. His second consecutive hat-trick in the tournament took him to seven career trebles in the competition – joint level with Messi.

CR7 was rested for the trip to lowly Granada, but returned to play in the last ever Madrid derby at the Vicente Calderon. The hosts raced into a 2-0 lead early on to spark hopes of a dramatic comeback, but another crucial goal from Isco following a great run from Benzema killed all hope of a home win.

With their place in Cardiff now guaranteed, Real turned their attention back to the league, and the visit of fourth-placed Sevilla. While Barcelona fans would have had hopes of a slip-up, Ronaldo stole the show once again with more broken records. His dynamite double took him clear of

400 goals for the club, and then in the next game at Celta Vigo, he broke Jimmy Greaves' 46-year record of most goals in Europe's top five leagues. More importantly, the win took Real Madrid clear of Barcelona at the top of the table, and left them needing just a point from their last game of the season.

Malaga offered little resistance, and after a wait of four seasons, Real finally had their hands back on the trophy. They became the first team in La Liga history to score in every single game of the season, and headed to the CL final brimming with confidence. After an even first half and a stunning equaliser from Mario Mandzukic, Real showed their class after the interval. Ronaldo's 600th goal in all competitions for club and country secured another Golden Boot in the tournament, as Los Blancos ran out comfortable winners. They became the first team in history to win consecutive Champions Leagues too, and confirmed their status as the greatest European club of all time.

It's party time at the end-of-season bus parade

REAL'S RESULTS

Date	Comp	Home	Score	Away
02/05	UCL	Real Madrid	3-0	Atletico Madrid
06/05	PRD	Granada	0-4	Real Madrid
10/05	UCL	Atletico Madrid	2-1	Real Madrid
14/05	PRD	Real Madrid	4-1	Sevilla
17/05	PRD	Celta Vigo	1-4	Real Madrid
21/05	PRD	Malaga	0-2	Real Madrid
03/06	UCL	Juventus	1-4	Real Madrid

STAT ATTACK!

Get a load of REAL MADRID's biggest signings, trophy cabinet, record scorers, Ballon d'Or winners and loads more!

FIVE BIGGEST SIGNINGS

	PLAYER	YEAR	FEE
1	Gareth Bale	2013	£85.3m
2	Cristiano Ronaldo	2009	£80m
3	James Rodriguez	2014	£63m
4	Kaka	2009	£56m
5	Zinedine Zidane	2001	£46m

FIVE BIGGEST SALES

	PLAYER	YEAR	FEE
1	Alvaro Morata	2017	£60m
2	Angel Di Maria	2014	£59.7m
3	Mesut Ozil	2013	£42.5m
4	Gonzalo Higuain	2013	£34.5m
5	Robinho	2008	£32.5m

MAJOR TROPHIES

12 Champions League

2 FIFA Club World Cup

3 Intercontinental Cup

2 Europa League

4 European Super Cup

33 La Liga

19 Copa del Rey

10 Spanish Super Cup

MOST APPEARANCES

Player		Apps
Raul	1994-2010	741
Iker Casillas	1999-2015	725
Manuel Sanchis	1983-2001	710
Santillana	1971-1988	645
Fernando Hierro	1989-2003	601
Francisco Gento	1953-1971	601
Jose Camacho	1973-1989	577
Pirri	1964-1980	561
Michel	1981-1996	559
Guti	1995-2010	542

7

Club legend Cristiano Ronaldo has scored 40 goals or more in all comps for the last seven seasons in a row – a Real Madrid record!

CHAMPIONS LEAGUE RECORD
ALL-TIME

PLAYED	WON
238	**142**

LOST	DRAWN
49	**47**

GOALS	CONCEDED
503	**255**

40 Between April 2016 and January 2017, Real Madrid went 40 games unbeaten in all competitions to set a new Spanish record!

ALL-TIME TOP SCORERS

- Emilio Butragueno 171
- Cristiano Ronaldo 406
- Pirri 172
- Karim Benzema 180
- Raul 323
- Francisco Gento 182
- Hugo Sanchez 208
- Alfredo Di Stefano 308
- Santillana 290
- Ferenc Puskas 242

0

Real Madrid are one of only three La Liga clubs – along with Barcelona and Athletic Bilbao – never to be relegated from La Liga!

9 Number of Real Madrid Ballon d'Or winners!

Alfredo Di Stefano 1957 & 1959	Ronaldo 2002
Raymond Kopa 1958	Fabio Cannavaro 2006
Luis Figo 2000	Cristiano Ronaldo 2013, 2014 & 2016

BIGGEST VICTORIES

LA LIGA HOME
11-2
v Elche, 1960

LA LIGA AWAY
2-8
v Deportivo, 2014

facebook
105+ MILLION Likes

twitter
25+ MILLION Followers

MARCELO
SAMBA STAR

Meet Marcelo... Real Madrid's Brazilian superhero!

Whether he's bombing up and down Real Madrid's left wing or bouncing around their changing room, Marcelo is always full of energy! The left-back has continued Los Blancos' tradition of attracting the best of Brazil, and has brought real Samba flair both on and off the pitch since he joined in 2007. The boy from Rio de Janeiro cost the club just £5.3 million, and ten years later has paid that fee back a hundred times over! With his wacky hairstyle and sense of fun, he's one of the most popular players at The Bernabeu, and backs it up with outstanding performances. With three appearances in the FIFA FIFPro World XI, there's no doubting him as one of the globe's very best full-backs.

THE NEW ROBERTO CARLOS

Madrid's No.12 arrived in the Spanish capital in January 2007, six months before club legend Roberto Carlos was to leave, and the two have been compared ever since. Although he doesn't have his hero's epic free-kick skills, Marcelo's attacking ability on the left flank has been a constant presence for Real over the past decade, just as Carlos' was for the previous eleven years before him.

REAL LEGEND

Although Roberto Carlos still holds the club's record for appearances by a foreign player, and the league record for a Brazilian, Marcelo isn't too far behind him. His trophy haul is just as impressive, too – the pair have each won three Champions Leagues and four La Ligas, with Marcelo getting onto the score sheet during the famous Decima win against Atletico in the 2014 final.

OFF THE PITCH

Marcelo isn't just a legend at Real for his quality displays on the pitch. He's one of the coolest players off it!

The years he's won the CL are engraved below his trophy tattoo

The Samba superstar knows tons of celebs

He's not just a baller in the football sense

His crazy Afro perfectly sums up his personality

adidas use him a lot to promote their products

REAL TROPHY CABINET

3x Champions Leagues

4x La Ligas

2x Club World Cups

2x Copas del Rey

3x Spanish Super Cups

3x European Super Cups

REAL MADRID BRAIN-BUSTER!

How well do you know the Spanish giants?

1. Real Madrid's away kit last season has been blacked out in this pic – what colour was it?

2. What nationality is flying full-back Marcelo?

3. In what year did France centre-back Raphael Varane make his debut for the club?

4. Who is Real Madrid's awesome head coach?

5. What shirt number does midfielder Isco wear – No.11, No.22 or No.33?

6. What is The Bernabeu's total stadium capacity – under 90,000 or over 90,000?

7. How many Champions League titles have the club won – 11, 12 or 13?

8. Which English club did Real sign megastar Gareth Bale from?

9. When were the club formed – 1892, 1902 or 1912?

10. How many times has a Real Madrid player won the Ballon d'Or – six, eight or nine?

1 ....
2 ....
3 ....
4 ....
5 ....
6 ....
7 ....
8 ....
9 ....
10 ....

FACE IN THE CROWD

Can you spot ten current Real Madrid superstars in this picture? The players below are all in the Los Blancos crowd somewhere!

Dani Carvajal

Sergio Ramos

Raphael Varane

Cristiano Ronaldo

Karim Benzema

Gareth Bale

Marcelo

Casemiro

Luka Modric

Marco Asensio

ANSWERS
ON PAGE 60

GALACTICOS
REAL MADRID'S SUPERSTARS!

Throughout **REAL MADRID**'s history, they have always had the most exciting, most expensive and most famous footballers in the world!

Zizou is presented as a Real player

ZIDANES & PAVONES

In 2000, Florentino Perez was elected president of Real Madrid on the promise that he would bring the world's biggest names to The Bernabeu. He delivered straight away, breaking the transfer record to sign Luis Figo from Barcelona in one of the most controversial transfers of all time. But this was just the start. Perez wanted to build a team of 'Zidanes and Pavones' – world-class stars on record-breaking deals like Zinedine Zidane, alongside homegrown players like Francisco Pavon. This vision for the club was inspired by the great Real sides of the past, when players from all over the world represented the club, but also led to transfer records and star-studded line-ups. As more and more heroes arrived for bigger and bigger contracts, they became known as 'The Galacticos'.

ZINEDINE ZIDANE

After signing Figo, the Spanish giants went in search of the next best player in the world, and in 2001 they got their man. Having won the 1998 World Cup and Euro 2000 with all-conquering France, and losing to Real in the 1998 Champions League final, the classy playmaker joined from Juventus for £46 million – a deal that remained the world record transfer fee for a further eight years.

LUIS FIGO

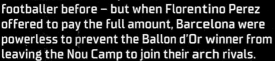

The Portugal wing wizard's transfer kick-started the new era of Galacticos. Figo's release clause at Barcelona stood at a monster £37.2 million – a figure that had never been paid for a footballer before – but when Florentino Perez offered to pay the full amount, Barcelona were powerless to prevent the Ballon d'Or winner from leaving the Nou Camp to join their arch rivals.

THE ORIGINAL GALACTICOS

DAVID BECKHAM

The most famous footballer in the world was the perfect signing for the most famous football club in the world. Becks' transfer in 2003 was the final addition to one of the most expensive line-ups of all time, and his reputation helped them sell over a million No.23 shirts around the world. But his footy ability was just as important, and his displays in 2006-07 were huge in bagging his only La Liga title.

RONALDO

Fresh from firing Brazil to the 2002 World Cup with eight goals, Ronaldo arrived for £29 million with a reputation as the world's No.1 striker. The fact he'd spent the 1996-97 season at Barcelona never bothered the Madridistas, and he was a hit with the fans from day one. Nicknamed 'The Phenomenon', he ended as the club's top scorer four years in a row and won the Pichichi in 2004.

GALACTICO RECORD BREAKERS

RAUL

Alongside Real's mega signings was a homegrown hero who cost nothing, yet Raul was possibly the team's biggest star of all. Signed from Atletico as a teen, he topped the club's all-time goals and appearance charts on his way to six La Ligas and three CLs. While other Galacticos came and went, Raul was a regular for 16 seasons, and remains one of the club's most popular players ever.

GARETH BALE

Real toppled the transfer record once again in 2013 when they swooped for Tottenham and Wales goal machine Gareth Bale. His pace, power and rocket shot drew obvious comparisons with the previous record-holder Ronaldo, and the combination of the two, alongside Karim Benzema, has given Real one of the most expensive and feared attacking trios of all time – BBC.

KAKA

In 2009, the club from the capital broke the world transfer record for a third time in a row by spending a mind-blowing £56 million on AC Milan midfielder Kaka. The last player apart from Messi or Ronaldo to win the Ballon d'Or moved to The Bernabeu with huge expectations, but a number of injuries meant that he rarely produced his best form, and returned to Milan after four seasons.

CRISTIANO RONALDO

Kaka's world-record fee lasted less than a month, before the La Liga giants smashed it again to sign C-Ron from Man. United. The ultimate Galactico completed the deal in style – his initial contract made him one of the highest-paid players in footy history, while his buy-out clause stood at a crazy €1 billion! Over the years, the signing has turned out to be an absolute bargain. Each of his 406 goals have cost Real under £200,000 – not to mention the countless trophies he's won for them!

JAMES RODRIGUEZ

When Rodriguez joined Real Madrid from Monaco for £63 million, only one other club had ever spent more on a player. The Colombia star really was a proper Galactico. Fresh from winning the Golden Boot at the 2014 World Cup in Brazil, the new No.10 was one of the most in-demand footballers on the planet, yet when Real came in for him, there was only ever one team he'd end up joining.

THE £150 MILLION LINE-UP

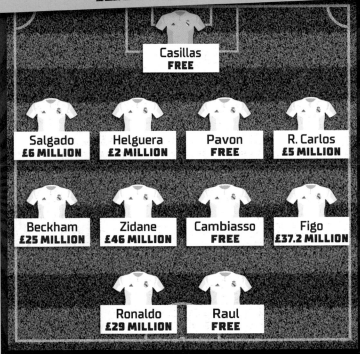

Casillas
FREE

Salgado
£6 MILLION

Helguera
£2 MILLION

Pavon
FREE

R. Carlos
£5 MILLION

Beckham
£25 MILLION

Zidane
£46 MILLION

Cambiasso
FREE

Figo
£37.2 MILLION

Ronaldo
£29 MILLION

Raul
FREE

Los Blancos' 2003 Spanish Super Cup clash with Mallorca saw them select one of the first XIs to cost over £150 million!

THE ORIGINAL LEGENDS

ALFREDO DI STEFANO

Before Cristiano Ronaldo smashed record after record, Alfredo Di Stefano was undoubtedly Real's greatest player ever. The ace forward was involved in a tug-of-war between Barça and Real, and by choosing Los Blancos, he was a hero in Madrid before even kicking a ball. After five European Cups and 308 goals in 396 games, he became an icon.

RAYMOND KOPA

Lining up alongside Di Stefano was France forward Raymond Kopa. After playing against Real in the 1956 European Cup Final, the attacker was snapped up by Los Blancos, and proceeded to win the next three trophies with the Spanish giants. He is one of only six players to win the Ballon d'Or while playing for Real Madrid.

FERENC PUSKAS

The final addition to Real's unstoppable attack in the '50s was Hungary star Puskas. He had already fired The Mighty Magyars to a World Cup Final before joining Real in 1958, and he went on to win three European Cups. He scored an incredible 242 goals in 262 games, and remains the only player ever to score hat-tricks in two European Cup Finals.

HUGO SANCHEZ

During the '80s, Real's biggest Galactico was Mexican striker Hugo Sanchez. Although the club failed to win a European Cup during his time in Spain, Sanchez's goals fired Real to five La Ligas from 1985 to 1990. He also won the Pichichi top scorer trophy outright four seasons in a row during this epic period, and he remains the only player to achieve this.

MODRIC
MIDFIELD MASTER

The maestro who gives the Real Madrid midfield oxygen.

In Spain, certain players are sometimes described as being able to give their teams oxygen, and nobody helps Real Madrid to breathe better than Croatia baller Luka Modric. From Carlo Ancelotti to Rafa Benitez and now Zinedine Zidane, the silky playmaker has been a favourite of all his Real Madrid managers, and it's so easy to see why. He has the control and technique to keep the ball glued to his boots, and the passing, vision and footy brain to unlock defences in the blink of an eye. More importantly, he connects the La Liga giants' rock-solid defence with their fearsome attack, and controls the tempo of games. While superstars Gareth Bale, Cristiano Ronaldo and Karim Benzema grab the headlines, it's pass master Modric that gives them the platform to be the stars.

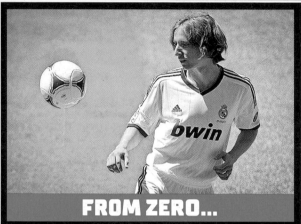

FROM ZERO...

Modric's Bernabeu career did not start well. Having missed much of pre-season, the Croatia star lacked the fitness of his rivals Xabi Alonso, Sami Khedira and Mesut Ozil, and was shifted around from left wing to attacking midfield. In December, he was voted the worst signing of the season by Madrid newspaper Marca, and a summer return to the Prem looked increasingly likely.

...TO HERO

Luka began to win the fans around in the second half of his debut season. In March, it was his corner that led to club legend Sergio Ramos' winner in El Clasico, and three days later he scored at Old Trafford to fire Real to the Champions League quarter-finals. From then, he began to stamp his mark on the team, starting all but one of the remaining La Liga games of the season.

BEZZIE BALE

The following summer, Modric was joined by his old Tottenham team-mate and PFA Player of the Year Gareth Bale in Madrid. Off the pitch, Luka helped the £85.3 million signing to settle, while their link-up play on the pitch was a key feature of Real's Copa del Rey and Champions League victories that season, with the two close friends playing starring roles in both finals.

CHAMPIONS LEAGUE STAR

The 2014 Champions League victory elevated the ace playmaker to new heights, and he has since gone on to become arguably one of the best midfielders in world football. He missed just three matches in Real's next two European successes, was named in the CL Team of the Tournament in each campaign, and is one of only five players to start in all three finals for Los Blancos.

MODRIC'S PASS ACCURACY

2016-17: 89.2%

2015-16: 90.9%

2014-15: 91.8%

2013-14: 90.8%

2012-13: 88.5%

ICONIC KITS!

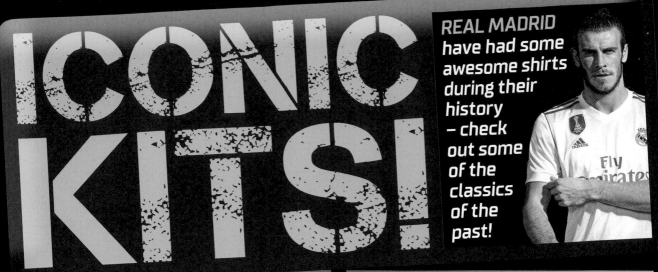

REAL MADRID have had some awesome shirts during their history – check out some of the classics of the past!

DID YOU KNOW?
Real suffered their biggest ever defeat in Europe in 1981-82, losing 5-0 to German side Kaiserslautern!

HOME 1981-82

Real Madrid kits don't get much more iconic than this! The 1981-82 jersey was the Spanish giants' first to be made by footy brand adidas, who are still making their kits to this day. Real's current deal with adidas has been running since 1998, with the German company paying them £850 million over the next ten years!

STAR MAN
Ivan Zamorano
Hitman Zamorano scored 28 La Liga goals in the 1994-95 season for Real – his best ever tally!

HOME 1994-95

Of course we were going to feature a Madrid shirt with dogs paws all over the sleeves! The mad kit, made by Spanish sports brand Kelme, helped Los Blancos to their first league title in five years and a 5-0 El Clasico win over Barcelona. It was the first Real shirt to be worn by legendary striker Raul, too.

STAT ATTACK
Real lost four times on their way to bagging the 1999-2000 CL – no team has ever lost more and won the famous trophy!

AWAY 1999-2000

The La Liga giants regularly wear black away kits, and this bad boy is one of their best ever. Not only did the gold trim ooze class, but the 12-times European champs wore it to bag their eighth Champions League crown. The club from the Spanish capital famously beat Man. United 3-2 at Old Trafford wearing it, too.

STAR MAN
Cristiano Ronaldo
The Portugal legend bagged 33 goals in just 35 games in all comps in his first season at The Bernabeu!

HOME 2009-10

Madridistas won't look back on this kit with many fond memories. Barcelona pipped them to the title despite racking up 96 points, and Ligue 1's Lyon surprisingly dumped them out of the CL at the last 16 stage. The cool kit was the first to be worn by Cristiano Ronaldo, though – and he's not done too badly at the club!

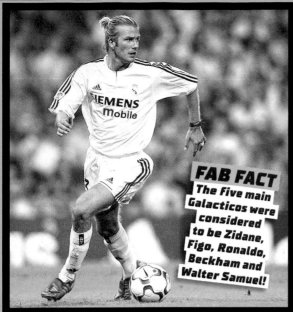

HOME 2003-04

A stylish shirt required stylish players, and that's exactly what Real had in the 2003-04 season. Dubbed 'The Galacticos', Madrid had a squad made up of Iker Casillas, Roberto Carlos, Zinedine Zidane, Raul, Ronaldo, Luis Figo, Ivan Helguera and David Beckham. It was one of the greatest teams to ever be assembled!

FAB FACT
The Five main Galacticos were considered to be Zidane, Figo, Ronaldo, Beckham and Walter Samuel!

MORE CLASSY KITS!

HOME 1960-61

THIRD 2004-05

THIRD 2011-12

This kit has been picked out for its beauty, rather than for the results Real got wearing it! It was Los Blancos' first red shirt since the 1970s, and was only used in away CL games. Jose Mourinho's Real crashed out at the semi-final stages though, so Madrid fans might not love it as much as you'd expect.

DID YOU KNOW?
Madrid didn't lose when wearing this kit in the Champo League!

THIRD 2013-14

FAB FACT
2014 was the last time Madrid won the Copa del Rey!

HOME 2013-14

Tons of top moments happened in this orange-trimmed number during the 2013-14 season. Cristiano Ronaldo hit a bonkers 51 goals in all comps, Gareth Bale scored THAT goal in the Copa del Rey Final against Barcelona and, of course, Real beat Atletico in the CL final to claim 'La Decima'. It was a victorious kit!

HOME 2000-01

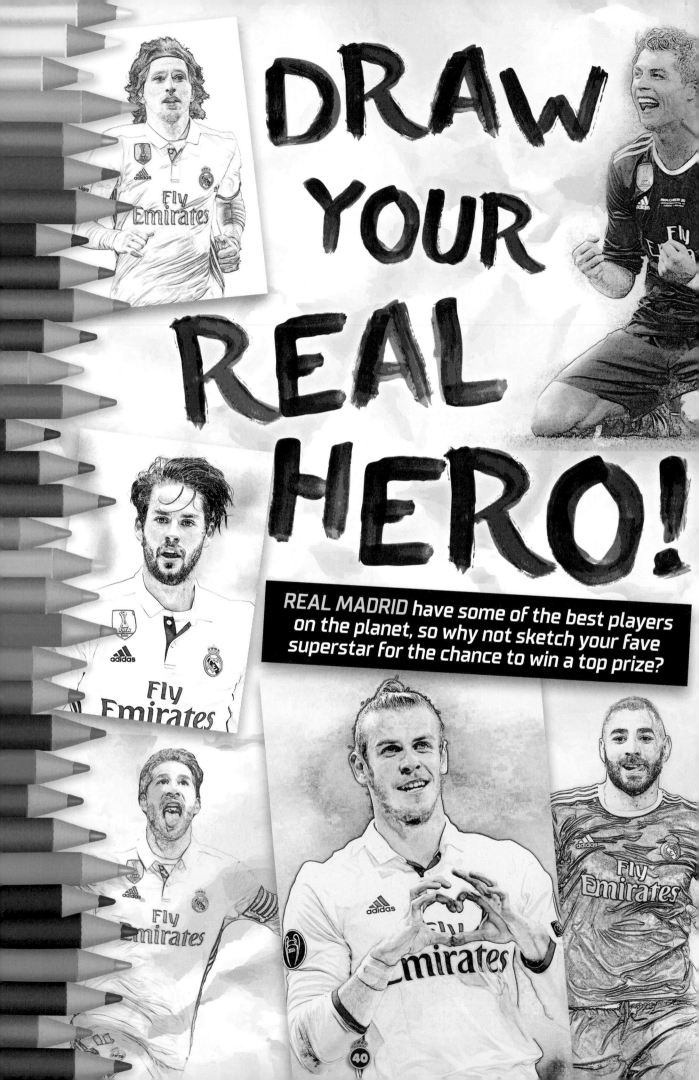

DRAW YOUR REAL HERO!

REAL MADRID have some of the best players on the planet, so why not sketch your fave superstar for the chance to win a top prize?

Name:

Date of birth:

Address:

Boot size:

Mobile:

Email:

KINGS OF

REAL MADRID did the double in 2016-17, including winning a 12th CL crown! Check out last season's record-breaking win in numbers, plus Madrid's history in footy's biggest club competition!

12 It was Real Madrid's 12th Champions League title – five more than nearest rivals AC Milan!

1 Los Blancos became the first team to retain the CL since the competition changed format in 1992!

27 Zinedine Zidane is the first boss to win back-to-back titles since Arrigo Sacchi in 1990 – 27 years ago!

EUROPE!

Juventus	1
Mandzukic 27	
Real Madrid	**4**
Ronaldo 20, 64; Casemiro 61; Asensio 90	

Just a fortnight after winning a record 33rd La Liga title, Real thumped Serie A champs Juventus to clinch a third CL crown in four seasons. Juve hitman Mario Mandzukic lit up the Principality Stadium in Cardiff with a sublime volley – one of the CL's all-time great final goals – but Cristiano Ronaldo ended up stealing the show, as usual, by firing the Spanish giants to European glory with a top-quality double!

600

After netting twice, Cristiano Ronaldo took his career goal tally for club and country to 600!

5

C–Ron's brace meant he finished as the Champo League's top scorer for the fifth season in a row!

TURN OVER FOR REAL'S CL WINS!

2015-16

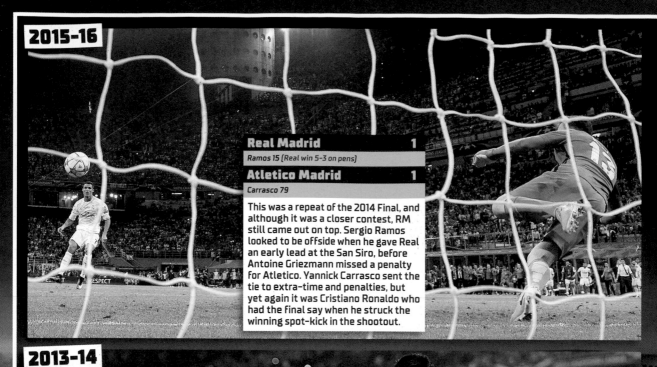

Real Madrid   **1**

Ramos 15 (Real win 5-3 on pens)

Atletico Madrid   **1**

Carrasco 79

This was a repeat of the 2014 Final, and although it was a closer contest, RM still came out on top. Sergio Ramos looked to be offside when he gave Real an early lead at the San Siro, before Antoine Griezmann missed a penalty for Atletico. Yannick Carrasco sent the tie to extra-time and penalties, but yet again it was Cristiano Ronaldo who had the final say when he struck the winning spot-kick in the shootout.

2013-14

Real Madrid   **4**

Ramos 90; Bale 110; Marcelo 118; Ronaldo 120 (pen)

Atletico Madrid   **1**

Godin 26 (After extra-time)

Real celebrated 'La Decima' after winning the first ever CL final between two teams from the same city, but it could have been so different. Atletico looked to be heading for victory thanks to Diego Godin's looping header, but Ramos' 93rd-minute goal sent the final to extra-time. Strikes by Gareth Bale, Marcelo and Ronaldo eventually won it for Real, and no-one will ever forget C-Ron's topless celebration!

2001-02

Bayer Leverkusen   **1**

Lucio 13

Real Madrid   **2**

Raul 8; Zidane 45

This final is remembered for one thing – Zinedine Zidane's mind-blowing volley that won the trophy at Hampden Park. After exchanging goals early on in the first half through Raul and Lucio, club ledge Zizou bagged the decisive strike when he volleyed Roberto Carlos' cross into the top corner from the edge of the penalty area. It's still regarded today as one of the greatest goals scored in Champions League history!

1999-2000

Real Madrid 3
Morientes 39; McManaman 67; Raul 75

Valencia 0

It was typical that Madrid, the CL's most successful team, would end up winning the first final of the new millennium. Steve McManaman's epic volley saw him become the first Englishman to win the CL with a foreign club, and it also marked the beginning of a great trophy haul – two La Liga titles and another CL in three years would follow!

1997-98

Juventus 0

Real Madrid 1
Mijatovic 66

Real ended a run of 32 years without a CL trophy with victory here. Juve were big faves – they were playing in their third final in a row, had just won a 25th Serie A title and had stars like Zidane, Edgar Davids and Alessandro Del Piero in their ranks – but striker Predrag Mijatovic's strike caused the upset!

1965-66

Real Madrid 2
Amancio 70; Serena 76

Partizan 1
Vasovic 55

1966 is a famous year in footy history, but Real remember it as the year they won back their European crown. They came from behind to beat Partizan 2-1 in Brussels, and it was fully deserved – they got to the final after scoring 19 goals in eight games against the likes of Inter, Anderlecht and Feyenoord!

1959-60

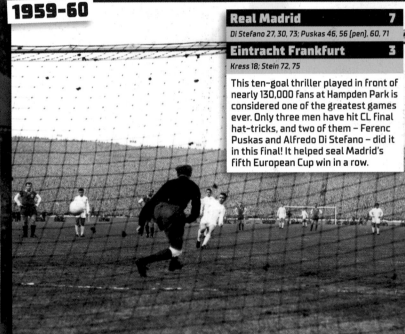

Real Madrid 7
Di Stefano 27, 30, 73; Puskas 46, 56 (pen), 60, 71

Eintracht Frankfurt 3
Kress 18; Stein 72, 75

This ten-goal thriller played in front of nearly 130,000 fans at Hampden Park is considered one of the greatest games ever. Only three men have hit CL final hat-tricks, and two of them – Ferenc Puskas and Alfredo Di Stefano – did it in this final! It helped seal Madrid's fifth European Cup win in a row.

1958-59

Real Madrid 2
Mateos 1; Di Stefano 47

Reims 0

Di Stefano continued his run of scoring in European Cup finals here as Real Madrid dominated French side Reims to claim a fourth European title. Heroes!

Real Madrid 3
Di Stefano 74; Rial 79; Gento 107

AC Milan 2
Schiaffino 59; Grillo 77 [After extra-time]

This was the first final to go to extra-time, with Spain and Real legend Francisco Gento netting the winner after yet another Di Stefano net-buster.

1957-58

Real Madrid 2
Di Stefano 69 (pen); Gento 75

Fiorentina 0

Real Madrid won their second European title by beating Italian side Fiorentina in front of 124,000 supporters at the Santiago Bernabeu stadium.

1956-57

Real Madrid 4
Di Stefano 14; Rial 30, 79; Marquitos 67

Reims 3
Leblond 6; Templin 10; Hidalgo 62

The first ever European Cup Final was an absolute classic! Real came from behind twice against Reims to win 4-3 at Paris' Parc des Princes.

1955-56

RAMOS

MR. MADRID

When Real need a hero, the Bernabeu legend normally steps up.

Ever since Sergio Ramos joined Real from Sevilla to become Spain's most expensive teenager ever, he's been one of the club's most important players, and there's no doubt the Spaniard has developed into one of the finest defenders of all time too. As well as being a proper tough tackler with bags of pace and strength, his ability on the ball allows him to play out from defence and help his team to build attacks. While his determination to win has at times gone too far – Ramos has been sent off more times than any other player in Real's history – his passion and leadership has made him a symbol of the club's success, and a real fans' favourite for the Madridistas. A knack for popping up and scoring crucial goals in the dying seconds of games just might have helped the skipper's popularity, too!

NEW HIERRO

After arriving in 2005 for £23.9 million, Ramos inherited the No.4 shirt from Fernando Hierro, the ex-captain who had won everything from the heart of Real's defence. The message was clear – Sergio was expected to fill the club legend's massive shoes, and become one himself. Even at the age of 19, the new boy rose to the challenge, and instantly became a key part of the Real team.

NATURAL LEADER

Over the following years, Ramos established himself as one of the world's top defenders, both on the right and in the centre of Real and Spain's back four. His status as a leader was cemented in 2009, when he was named as one of three vice-captains to club legend Raul. Six years later, Sergio was promoted to the full role, inspiring the club to two Champions League wins.

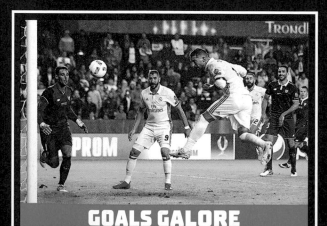

GOALS GALORE

As well as being a top defender, Ramos also has a habit of scoring crucial goals. Last season was his best display in front of goal with a total of ten, including five in the 80th minute or later. His equaliser in the 93rd minute of the UEFA Super Cup against Sevilla helped Real to their first trophy of the season, while late goals at home to Deportivo and Real Betis were key in the title win.

RIVAL SLAYER

Some of his finest moments in a white shirt have come against Real's biggest rivals. His last-minute equaliser at the Nou Camp last season was huge in the title race, and he's also beaten Barça in two Copa del Rey finals. His stoppage-time header in the all-Madrid 2014 CL Final saved Real from defeat too, while his goal in the 2016 repeat helped him collect the Man of the Match award.

REAL TROPHY CABINET

3x Champions Leagues

4x La Ligas

2x Club World Cups

2x Copas del Rey

3x Spanish Super Cups

3x European Super Cups

47

WORDFIT

Can you fit the Real Madrid legends into the giant grid below?

ROBERTOCARLOS

Benito	Cunningham	Mateos	Raul	Santillana
Bernabeu	Del Bosque	McManaman	Roberto Carlos	Seedorf
Butragueno	Di Stefano	Michel	Ronaldo	Suker
Camacho	Gento	Morientes	Salgado	Valdano
Cannavaro	Guti	Pirri	Sanchez	Zamorano
Casillas	Hierro	Puskas	Sanchis	Zidane

NAME THE TEAM

The stars from Real Madrid's 2017 Champions League Final win over Juventus are hiding – can you work out who they are?

1. Goalkeeper

2. Centre-back

3. Midfielder

4. Centre-back

5. Striker

6. Forward

7. Defensive midfielder

8. Left-back

9. Right-back

10. Attacking midfielder

11. Midfielder

ANSWERS ON PAGE 60

ALL-TIME FUT LEGENDS

With the release of brand-new FUT Icons on FIFA 18, we check out what made some past REAL MADRID Legends on FIFA's Ultimate Team so legendary! Check them all out...

BUTRAGUENO

1982-1995
Games: 463 ★ Goals: 171

90 ST		
BUTRAGUEÑO		
91 PAC	87 DRI	
88 SHO	36 DEF	
78 PAS	65 PHY	
BASIC		

Skilful striker Emilio Butragueno was a boyhood Real fan. Nicknamed 'The Vulture', he was the leader of five homegrown heroes known as 'The Vulture Squad' that formed the spine of Real's team in the '80s and '90s!

REAL HONOURS

La Liga	6
UEFA Cup	2
Copa del Rey	2
Spanish Super Cup	4
Spanish League Cup	1

HIERRO

1989-2003
Games: 601 ★ Goals: 127

89 CB		
HIERRO		
70 PAC	72 DRI	
67 SHO	89 DEF	
70 PAS	83 PHY	
BASIC		

Fernando Hierro was a solid yet skilful CB with an eye for a pass, and captained Real through one of their best periods. He hit over 100 goals for Los Blancos, including 26 in one season, and ended his career as Spain's record scorer too!

REAL HONOURS

Champions League	3
La Liga	5
UEFA Super Cup	1
Copa del Rey	1
Spanish Super Cup	4
Intercont. Cup	2

LAUDRUP

1994-96
Games: 76 ★ Goals: 15

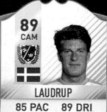

89 CAM		
LAUDRUP		
85 PAC	89 DRI	
73 SHO	38 DEF	
87 PAS	64 PHY	
BASIC		

Michael Laudrup was a hit with the Real fans before kicking a ball after leaving Barça to sign, but within a year became a total legend. By winning the league in his first season, he helped end Barça's four-year title streak. He was a baller!

REAL HONOURS

La Liga	1

FIGO

2000-05
Games: 163 ★ Goals: 38

90
RW

FIGO

83 PAC	90 DRI
81 SHO	38 DEF
86 PAS	75 PHY

BASIC

Luis Figo's decision to leave Barcelona for Real was one of the most controversial transfers ever. But it made the silky winger a hero to the Madridistas just like Laudrup. The record signing won the Ballon d'Or in his debut season at the club!

REAL HONOURS

Champions League	1
La Liga	2
UEFA Super Cup	1
Spanish Super Cup	2
Intercont. Cup	1

VAN NISTELROOY

2006-10
Games: 96 ★ Goals: 64

90
ST

NISTELROOY

84 PAC	76 DRI
89 SHO	33 DEF
68 PAS	76 PHY

BASIC

Lethal Ruud van Nistelrooy was a real poacher – he hit 25 goals in his first season, including four in one match, seven in consecutive games and almost all inside the penalty area! That bagged him the Pichichi trophy and helped fire Real to the title.

REAL HONOURS

| La Liga | 2 |
| Spanish Super Cup | 1 |

ROBERTO CARLOS

1996-2007
Games: 527 ★ Goals: 68

Roberto Carlos had the pace, energy, and attacking quality to control the left side of the pitch all by himself. He was famous for his long-range shots and free-kicks, and played more times for Real than any other non-Spaniard.

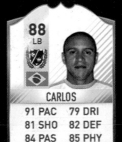

88
LB

CARLOS

91 PAC	79 DRI
81 SHO	82 DEF
84 PAS	85 PHY

BASIC

REAL HONOURS

Champions League	3
La Liga	4
UEFA Super Cup	1
Spanish Super Cup	3
Intercont. Cup	2

CANNAVARO

2006-09
Games: 106 ★ Goals: 1

89
CB

CANNAVARO

73 PAC	65 DRI
39 SHO	91 DEF
57 PAS	81 PHY

BASIC

REAL HONOURS

| La Liga | 2 |
| Spanish Super Cup | 1 |

Top leader Fabio Cannavaro lifted the 2006 Ballon d'Or after captaining Italy to the World Cup, and joined Real in the same year. Madrid won back-to-back league titles in the defender's first two seasons, and he's still one of their finest ever CBs.

OWEN

2004-05
Games: 45 ★ Goals: 16

88
ST

OWEN

89 PAC	86 DRI
85 SHO	22 DEF
67 PAS	64 PHY

BASIC

REAL HONOURS

None

A pacy predator, Michael Owen cost Real £8 million from Liverpool in 2004. Although he couldn't break into the team ahead of Raul and Ronaldo, the England ace ended his only season in Spain with the best mins-to-goal ratio at the club.

REAL MADRID'S TOP 10 EL CLASICO MOMENTS!

Check out some of REAL MADRID's best ever moments against their massive rivals Barcelona!

'10 CARLOS' CORKER!
Real Madrid 3-0 Barcelona
La Liga, 2000

Roberto Carlos scored some epic FKs during his career, but he saved one of his best for this El Clasico match-up. He let fly from 35 yards after just five minutes, with the ball crashing into the far corner!

9 MESSI v RONALDO!
Barcelona 2-2 Real Madrid
La Liga, 2012

Many consider this match as the Clasico where both Lionel Messi and Cristiano Ronaldo showcased their world-class talents. They both scored twice, with CR7 bagging in a sixth El Clasico in a row. Legend!

8 AWESOME ARAGON!
Real Madrid 4-1 Barcelona
Spanish Super Cup, 1990

Santiago Aragon only played 18 times for Real, so this game defines his Madrid career. RM were cruising to a 3-1 win, but Aragon didn't think Barça's humiliation was complete, so he sensationally lobbed the goalkeeper from the halfway line!

7 REAL LOVE CHIPS!
Barcelona 0-2 Real Madrid
Champions League, 2002

Real were struggling in La Liga in 2001-02, but in the CL they were a different beast! In this semi-final first leg, Zinedine Zidane and Steve McManaman scored two chips to give Real a 2-0 win. Barça never recovered, and RM won a record ninth CL title a month later!

DI STEFANO'S DEADLY DEBUT!
Real Madrid 5-0 Barcelona
La Liga, 1953

In 1953, Real and Barça weren't just battling it out on the pitch – but off it too. They were both chasing footy legend Alfredo Di Stefano's signature, with Madrid coming out on top. Two days after signing, Di Stefano was lining up against Barça and showed them what they missed out on by scoring twice!

5 GUARD OF HONOUR!
Real Madrid 4-1 Barcelona
La Liga, 2008

This match will live long in the memory for Real fans! Madrid had won La Liga in their last game, so Barcelona formed a guard of honour as Los Blancos' title-winners walked onto the pitch. It got even more embarrassing for Barça, as Raul and co. hit four past them!

4 RON RISES HIGH!
Barcelona 0-1 Real Madrid
Copa del Rey, 2011

In 2010-11, there were four Clasicos in the space of 17 days – La Liga, the Copa del Rey final and CL semis. In the Copa, Madrid came out on top thanks to an epic Ronaldo header. He rose high in extra-time to nod the ball home, as Jose Mourinho finally got the better of Pep Guardiola!

3 GARETH THE GREAT!
Real Madrid 2-1 Barcelona
Copa del Rey, 2014

This was the night Gareth Bale came of age as a Real player! With five minutes to play, the Wales ace got the ball inside his own half. He put the burners on and ran 65 yards upfield, sprinting around Marc Barta off the pitch, then into the box before slotting the ball home!

2 MANITA MAGIC!
Real Madrid 5-0 Barcelona
La Liga, 1995

This 5-0 win for Madrid, La Manita in Spanish, marked a changing of the guard in Spain – Barça had bossed La Liga for four years bagging title after title. Ivan Zamorano hit a treble, while ex-Barça man Michael Laudrup dominated the game. It set Real on their way to their 26th title!

1 COOL CRISTIANO!
Barcelona 1-2 Real Madrid
La Liga, 2012

After three La Liga titles in a row, Real were desperate to end Barça's dominance – and after inflicting a home defeat on their rivals for the first time in 55 games, the title was all but secured. Ronaldo coolly netted the winner, and his iconic 'calm down' celebration at the Nou Camp will never be forgotten!

RONALDO
RECORD BREAKER

Cristiano Ronaldo doesn't break records – he totally shatters them!

Since moving to Madrid in 2009, Ron's ticked off almost every record in his path. He overtook Real's previous top goalscorer Raul in 431 fewer games on his way to racking up tons of trophies and individual awards. Check out some of his greatest ever achievements...

FIRST-CLASS RECORDS

Ronaldo is the first player in history to...

Score in every minute of a game

Score 60 goals in a calendar year four times in a row

Win the league title, Champions League, domestic Super Cup, Golden Shoe, Ballon d'Or, Club World Cup and domestic cup with two teams

Score in Champions League finals for two different winning clubs

REAL MADRID RECORDS

406 The club's all-time leading scorer

21 Top scorer in the Madrid derby

4 Joint-highest European Golden Shoe award winner

LEAGUE RECORDS

369 Most league goals across Europe's top five divisions

32 Most hat-tricks in La Liga history

58 Most penalties scored in La Liga

EUROPEAN RECORDS

105 Most goals scored in Champo League history

11 Most UEFA Team of the Year appearances

6 Most Champo League top scorer awards

REAL TROPHY CABINET

3x Champions Leagues
2x La Ligas
2x Club World Cups
2x Copas del Rey
2x Spanish Super Cup
2x European Super Cup

CR7 BOOT HISTORY

Get a load of all the awesome CR7 signature paint jobs CRISTIANO RONALDO's had on his Nike Mercurial kicks!

YEAR: 2010
Hit a total of 19 goals for the La Liga giants in his debut signature boot!

YEAR: 2011
Scored the winning goal in the 2011 Copa del Rey Final wearing these!

YEAR: 2011
These had bits of red on them, but they were used to beat rivals Atletico!

YEAR: 2012
Helped C-Ron become the first star to score in six consecutive Clasicos!

YEAR: 2013
These awesome kicks looked sick in the all-white of Real Madrid!

YEAR: 2013
This crazy red, black, yellow and white paint job was well memorable!

YEAR: 2013
Scored his 100th away goal in his 106th away appearance for Madrid!

YEAR: 2014
The gold celebrated the goal machine winning his first Ballon d'Or at Real!

YEAR: 2014
We reckon you'll agree these were one of the classiest CR7 cleats ever!

YEAR: 2015
Yep, you guessed it – more gold celebrated another Ballon d'Or win!

YEAR: 2015
Hit five goals in one league game for the first time in his epic career!

YEAR: 2015
It was only right he became Madrid's all-time top scorer in white boots!

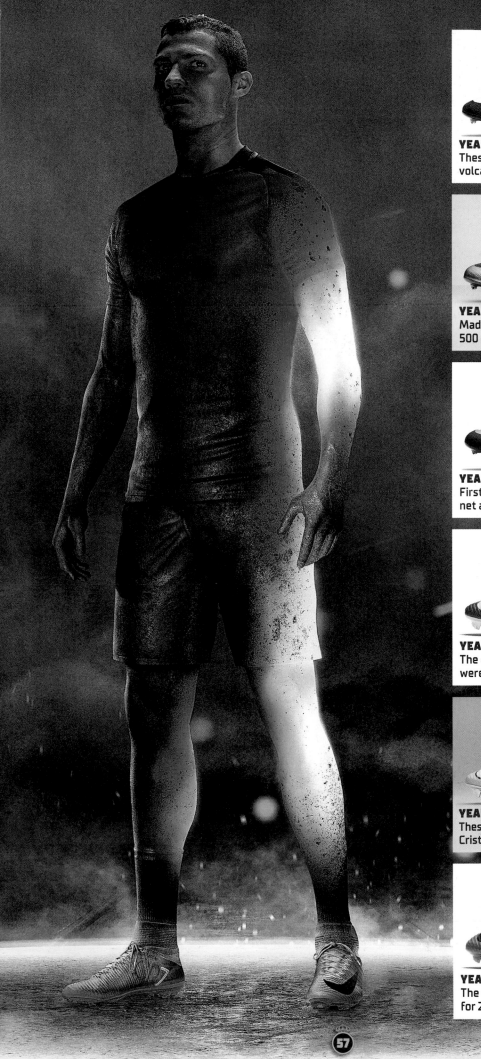

YEAR: 2015
These were inspired by Madeira, the volcanic island where Ron was born!

YEAR: 2016
Made to commemorate Ron reaching 500 career goals for club and country!

YEAR: 2016
First time he wore these, he ripped net against arch rivals Barcelona!

YEAR: 2016
The colours on these quality cleats were inspired by First club Sporting!

YEAR: 2016
These limited-edition kicks celebrated Cristiano's mind-blowing form in 2016!

YEAR: 2017
The heel had the Roman numerals for 28, Ronaldo's first shirt number!

2017-18 FIRST TEAM SQUAD

GOALKEEPERS

No.	Player	La Liga Games/Goals 2016-17	Signed From
1	Keylor Navas	27/0	Levante, 2014
13	Kiko Casilla	11/0	Espanyol, 2015

Keylor Navas

DEFENDERS

No.	Player	La Liga Games/ Goals 2016-17	Signed From
2	Dani Carvajal	23/0	B. Leverkusen, 2013
3	Jesus Vallejo	N/A	Real Zaragoza, 2015
4	Sergio Ramos	28/7	Sevilla, 2005
5	Raphael Varane	23/1	Lens, 2011
6	Nacho	28/2	Academy
12	Marcelo	30/2	Fluminense, 2007
15	Theo Hernandez	N/A	Atletico, 2017
19	Achraf Hakimi	N/A	Academy

Marcelo

Isco

MIDFIELDERS

No.	Player	La Liga Games/Goals 2016-17	Signed From
8	Toni Kroos	29/3	Bayern Munich, 2014
10	Luka Modric	25/1	Tottenham, 2012
14	Casemiro	25/4	Sao Paulo, 2013
18	Marcos Llorente	N/A	Academy
20	Marco Asensio	23/3	Mallorca, 2014
22	Isco	30/10	Malaga, 2013
23	Mateo Kovacic	27/1	Inter, 2015
24	Dani Ceballos	N/A	Real Betis, 2017

Lucas Vazquez

FORWARDS

No.	Player	La Liga Games/Goals 2016-17	Signed From
7	Cristiano Ronaldo	29/25	Man. United, 2009
9	Karim Benzema	29/11	Lyon, 2009
11	Gareth Bale	19/7	Tottenham, 2013
17	Lucas Vazquez	33/2	Academy
21	Borja Mayoral	N/A	Academy

MEET THE MANAGER...

ZINEDINE ZIDANE

Country: France

D.O.B: 23 June, 1972

Former Club: Real Madrid B

Honours: 2x Champions Leagues, 1x La Liga, 1x FIFA Club World Cup, 2x European Super Cups, 1x Spanish Super Cup

Top players don't always make great managers, but Zidane is one of the best exceptions to that rule. As Real's midfield maestro, he was a star and one of the most skilful players of the 21st century. His spectacular volley sealed the 2002 CL final, but after retiring four years later, he wasn't tipped as a future boss.

The Frenchman has proved his doubters wrong, though! Zizou learned from legendary manager Carlo Ancelotti as his assistant at Real for a season, before being given his chance in 2014 as gaffer of the B team. After the sacking of then Bernabeu manager Rafa Benitez in 2016, Zidane took over as the new Los Blancos boss!

His knowledge of the club and man-management skills have allowed him to get the very best out of his players, and his record of seven trophies already speaks for itself! Zidane could be the first long-term manager Real Madrid have had for a very long time.

Wordsearch P14

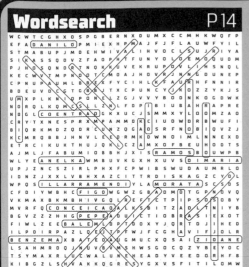

Brain-Buster P30

1. Purple

2. Brazilian

3. 2011

4. Zinedine Zidane

5. No.22

6. Under 90,000

7. 12

8. Tottenham

9. 1902

10. Nine

Name The Team P49

1. Keylor Navas

2. Sergio Ramos

3. Toni Kroos

4. Raphael Varane

5. Karim Benzema

6. Cristiano Ronaldo

7. Casemiro

8. Marcelo

9. Dani Carvajal

10. Isco

11. Luka Modric

Spot The Difference P15

Wordfit P48

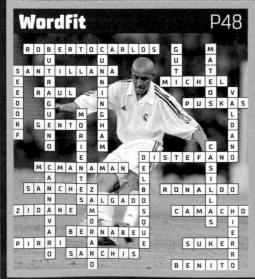

Face In The Crowd P31

ROLL OF HONOUR

FIFA CLUB OF THE CENTURY
2000

CHAMPIONS LEAGUE
1955-56, 1956-57, 1957-58, 1958-59, 1959-60,
1965-66, 1997-98, 1999-00, 2001-02, 2013-14,
2015-16, 2016-17

FIFA CLUB WORLD CUP
2014, 2016

INTERCONTINENTAL CUP
1960, 1998, 2002

UEFA CUP
1984-85, 1985-86

EUROPEAN SUPER CUP
2002, 2014, 2016, 2017

LA LIGA
1931-32, 1932-33, 1953-54, 1954-55, 1956-57,
1957-58, 1960-61, 1961-62, 1962-63, 1963-64,
1964-65, 1966-67, 1967-68, 1968-69, 1971-72,
1974-75, 1975-76, 1977-78, 1978-79, 1979-80,
1985-86, 1986-87, 1987-88 1988-89, 1989-90,
1994-95, 1996-97, 2000-01, 2002-03, 2006-07,
2007-08, 2011-12, 2016-17

COPA DEL REY
1904-05, 1905-06, 1906-07, 1907-08, 1916-17,
1933-34, 1935-36, 1945-46, 1946-47, 1961-62,
1969-70, 1973-74, 1974-75, 1979-80, 1981-82,
1988-89, 1992-93, 2010-11, 2013-14

SPANISH SUPER CUP
1988, 1989, 1990, 1993, 1997, 2001, 2003, 2008,
2012, 2017

SPANISH LEAGUE CUP
1984-85

SMALL WORLD CUP
1952, 1956

LATIN CUP
1955, 1957

REGIONAL CHAMPIONSHIP
1903-04, 1904-05, 1905-06, 1906-07, 1907-08,
1912-13, 1915-16, 1916-17, 1917-18, 1919-20, 1921-22,
1922-23, 1923-24, 1925-26, 1926-27, 1928-29,
1929-30, 1930-31

MANCOMUNADOS TROPHY
1931-32, 1932-33, 1933-34, 1934-35, 1935-36

COPA IBEROAMERICANA
1994

EVA DUARTE CUP
1947